MW01526299

Pilgrims of Zame

A Collection of Hybrid Narratives

Mbizo Chirasha

Publisher:

Footprints Publishing House

P.O. Box 30162

Chichiri

Blantyre

Malawi

Cell: +265 884 137 788

Email: fpublishinghouse@gmail.com

© Mbizo Chirasha 2021

All rights reserved. No part of this book may be reproduced or transmitted in any form or by any means, mechanical or electronic, including photocopying and recording, or be stored in any information storage or retrieval system, without written permission from the publisher or the author.

TABLE OF CONTENTS

iv

DEDICATION

Dedicated to all Zimbabweans, Africans and global citizens speaking freedom, justice, peace and unity.

FOREWORD

In **Pilgrims of Zame: A Collection of Hybrid Narratives,** *Mbizo Chirasha first takes the reader to Zimbabwe for a spiritual celebration, to which the congregants bring their supplication for rain.*

Here, millet beer flows freely and wafts the aroma of bread. "Men [sit] on leopard skin mats and women [sit] on sheepskin." Nuns dance with a dignity that is written into the variety of the shapes of their creation.

Today, as I read and write about Chirasha's narratives, my desk looks out onto a cold and wintry Canadian scene. Our places on this earth couldn't be more different. And yet, the writer, the poet, the griot from Zimbabwe moves a mighty pen as he brings the warmth of his country all the way here, to the Northern Rocky Mountains of my home.

This—bridging the space between continents—is one of Chirasha's many gifts.

In "Letters to God," he reveals the poetic soul of an environmentalist as he writes:

"When the red glow of heat persisted like in hell. Silence and barrenness are weaved together onto red earth. While rivers become white washed skeletons of dry sand. Elders spoke in tongues to the wind... They are told to wash their feet and dance to Gods. They were punished for replacing forests with concrete jungles. Birds and spirits of the land were now vagabonds. They are told the earth is simmering in abomination and Gods are angry and choked with carbon laced fumes. They are warned of the coming of devil's triplets: hunger, heat waves and cyclones. They paid their ornaments, applauded the gods and returned to their hovels underneath the fringes of Zvagona hills."

But it is not the poverty-stricken here, the ones housed in hovels, who are to blame, and we see the unfairness of the gods' judgement on those who only ask for rain.

And then the rain comes.

"Midnight City," finds the author "Downtown under the old bridge, [where] (d) elinquent boys, serial drunks, life rejects

atitution and rape are driven by poverty and corruption. Because "(h)ere is where political players deposit the country's future in pink bras. Mugs of cheap whisky castrate city leaders into useless imbeciles."

In Pilgrims of Zame, celebration and violence erupt on the same page:

"[The] new year boomed to life with cheap firecrackers, sparking the heavens open for blessings. The faint scent of Christmas had vanished, long since fading into the burning heat. The latest music vibrated the entire village. We enjoyed so many assorted meats, their tastes were all as one in our mouths. Fanta and Coca Cola drinks soaked our okra-hardened bellies. We ate English and drank American that day...

"Yes, our joyful morning went by with its gossip-beat; the afternoon elapsed with sweet odors of roasted meat and sunset shadows, and then, the once-silent Mandoza took over our night by spewing gunshots, death threats, and insults."

Celebration and violence are hand-in-glove in this collection. And through it, like an aroma permeating its pages, we discover the author's love for his country, as infused into these stories as the scent of roasting meat.

Darcie Friesen Hossack, a Multi Award Winning Writer , Storyteller. Associate Editor of Time of the Poet Republic. Managing Editor of WordCityMonthly. CommonWealth Prize Nominee. Her story "Little Lamb" was nominated for the 2008 McClelland & Stewart Journey Prize.

PILGRIMS OF ZAME

A harsh heave of shrine incense combined with the stink of
ancient snuff and herbal concoctions choked our lungs. The
smell was new and strange. The evening was pleated with
defiant black shadows and mismatched silhouettes of small
hills. Everything was stitched together by instructive
spiritual incantations and strange guttural bellows. Angels
warmed drums on live embers. Mediums roared in
synchronized incantations.
"Heyi hii hoo
Heyi hii hoo"
They unstoppably shook their heads and trembled their
shoulders from one trance into another. Dust swirls aroused
from their dances carried our blessings. The mist that
shrouded the grey hills carried the anointing of the land.
They guzzled the millet brew in their order of seniority.
Worshippers had brought large pots of millet beer from our
villages. The ceremonial beer was brewed and brought to
the shrine gallery by pre-pubescent and post-menopausal
women. That was to ensure that the shrine's sacredness is
maintained

1

Matonjeni hills were shrouded in silence and draped in long gowns of grey mist at dawn. During evenings,hills were hugged by apostolic like plain white robes of mist again. Zame is known of bone chilling spits of drizzle year in and year out. We arrived before shadows fully quilted the earth. We didn't bring modern utensils and blankets into the hills. We walked with our barefoot. Men sat on leopard skin mats and women sat on sheepskin.

Drapes of mist grew the hills into a shrine of black shadows. The moon set like a silver arc over the rim of the mystic Malindidzimu "the seat of gods". It was gorgeous. It winked to us behind a veil of fluffy, white and smoky drizzling clouds. Soft rains caressed our day long sun-drained skins.

Malindidzimu is the zenith of Zame, the place where gods sit to watch the earth underneath them. When night is ripe the silver moon winks to the gods to take rest. Mermaids are said to wash gods's feet in Mavulamachena, the gorge of white waters situated at the fontanel of Malindidzimu. The waters are ever silver moon white.The mist rises from

2

Mavulamachena "white waters" to dress the sacred mountains with white skirts and grey doeks towards dawn. When the world is trapped in the web of sleep, gods are said to float along with mist drapings to meet with their earthly ambassadors. The mystery of Matonjeni, shrine of gods.

The Matonjeni gallery sits somewhere on a mountain range that runs from east to west. The shrine entrances wind up and down among overhung granite boulders into the gallery. We washed our feet upon entering the shrine to do away with dust and bad omen. Every visitor was blessed with portion of ancient snuff before entering the shrine. The scent of snuff was strange. I sneezed and drooled like a wild pig.That was the same with my fellow congregants. The snuff was strong. After the ritual, eunuchs and nuns led us into the shrine. The shrine is an art gallery with a unique spiritual presence. Gallery walls were beautifully decorated

with red and black clay earth extracted from the nearby

termite mounds, the lush and green combat that dressed the anthills added ambiance to this astounding earthly but spiritual wonderment. A plethora of ornaments that included animal horns, bone-made trinkets, grass-made beads and ancient spears made up the Matonjeni gallery collection. The exhibition was diligently curated. The gallery walls were stripped with white, red, black clay patterns. After our maiden tour, we then supplicated to God with a thunderous chorus of applause and heart-rending, mountain cave-echoing ululations. We thanked gods and spirits for guiding us from evil during our long day journey to the holy land.

The Hallowed eunuch of the shrine, Nyamasviswa with his band of Matonjeni disciples welcomed us with that verve of spiritual merriment. The dignifying gesture uplifted our sun-burnt, day-long trip-tired souls. We brought large pots frothing with millet beer. It was abundant, plenty more than what other clansmen had brought. The traditional millet brew smelt like freshly baked bread. Mediums salivated with that greedily gusto, waiting impatiently to feast from the mouth-watering pots frothing the ancient delicacy. It was intelligently brewed by earth-scratching, peasantry lifestyle-hardened hands, thus combined with the verve of ancestral wisdom passed from one matriarchal epoch to more and more other matriarchal generations. The welcoming merriment was remote paused by a blood-splashing hymn, divinely echoed from a swarm of beautiful nuns as it passionately coiled into our groping hearts. We got spiritually connected to the land that carried the bones, breath and promise of our fathers. The wild dove-hen crowing like alto voices pleated our static black silhouettes, the tinkering tenor of throbbing drums, discordant snores of sleeping waters and the vibe of human mass together onto the hems of mystic hills

Dzinomwa kuna runde

Mhondoro dzinomwa a a

Dzinomwa kunaSave

Mhondoro Dzinomwa...a...a a a

Dzinomwa kuna rundee

Mhondoro dzinomwa AAA

The shrine suddenly slid into an abrupt frenzy of traditional dance-songs and a poetic trance of ancestral praise. The scantily dressed nuns danced until their slim frames soaked in sweat. Their rotund figures were clad in different regalia made of goatskin, leopard and lion skins and other beautifying paraphernalia. They received their costumes in accordance with their levels of seniority and nature of duties. These maidservants were all beautiful but well trained to charge their duties with due diligence and requisite zeal. It was like they were born from one big womb, we found it difficult to distinguish them, and they looked alike as black-eyed peas and they carried themselves with that high calibre of moral consciousness and hyperbolised dignity. Their body frames were a real fulfilment of god's unmatched creativity. Their breasts were taunt and straight like porcupine quills ready to spike, as they quivered like turgid, fresh ripe mangoes ready to fall from their mother tree. Our untamed hearts skipped to suffocate us, the amazing beauty that blinded both brave hunters and seasoned dancers among other revellers. Male congregants had to tame their manhood because the temptations were extreme, beyond human reasoning and above sexual-emotional control. We uncontrollably salivated at the rawness of that unspoilt human dignity. The wonder-angels were all virgins, they had under gone a traditional initiation including sacrificial oaths to be maid servants of the holy land. That they would never become wives, mothers or indulge into any intercourse of sexual nature until the time of their demise. They carried their chores with profound zeal and well calculated precision. Their service varied according to age, clan of origin, talent, teachings, practice and seniority.

The appearance of Dungwiza, the rainmaking medium interrupted the current mood. His elephantine frame was draped in an unusual all black apparel. The baritone-gifted man boasted of his gigantic frame and ever darting eyes that never blinked to anything. A sign of bravery. He waved and yawned thrice, the drumming, the chanting an dancing stopped abruptly. The night was still young. Dungwiza was the leader of main rituals including rainmaking occasions at Matonjeni. The gallery slid into an abrupt silence like at graveyard. Dungwiza made a rushed stride towards the epicenter of the shrine. Maidservants ululated like cooing doves praise and worshipping the last rays of setting sun.

Dungwiza blew three full finger pinches of ancient snuff and then wiped black snort with the back of his aged and weather-toughened hands. The rustling sound of stubborn winds was drowned by the beat of his poetic incantations.

Imwi mhondoro dzenyika

Varidzi vepasi nemuronga wenyu

Ndauya kuzosuma pwere dzenyu

Nyika yapinda munzamusha

Musha waparara nehosha
Musha wovava segavaka
Pasi ronhuwhwa segutukutu
Vana vayaura, pasi raoma roda veta
Vana vofa nenyota vodzungaira

Dzorai moyo, musasunga moyo

Nyika yoda donhodzo vana vagute

Vanayaura, vafamba mitunhu kuzochema kwamuri

Mukai muone misodzi yavo netarisiro.

Vana vasingachemi vanofira mumbereko

The spirited supplications were punctuated by yawns, bellows and sneezing from shrine disciples and other

8

mediums. Plumes of burning incense and whiffs of black snuff conquered the shrine the scent was both suffocating and beautiful. The rainmaking prayer was capped by an electric echo of ululations from the band of Matonjeni nuns. The shrine was lit with spiritual blaze and human rhythm. Dungwiza tossed his Muhacha rod upwards. He ordered drummers to beat the Shangana neShumba drum. Drums were cracked and their throb vibrated the land. The rhythm was tense and beat was unmatched. Behold the land was holy.

Suddenly, spats of drizzle grew fat, heavens opened their floodgates, and heavy rain soaked the earth. Drums tinkered still. The night was now aging and was clad in a dark grey gown preparing to surrender Matonjeni shrine to the angels of dawn. Dawn proudly winked its twilight for the elephants to rise from slumber and take an early morning bath,Nguva dzamashambanzou. Mediums sneezed from one trance to another. We chanted still, we sang still and danced still. The rhythm of our dance and song traversed to the lands faraway and reached onto the holy ears of gods.

The eastern hills wore an orange monkey hat and ochre–red blood robe, wiping off mist from the rain–thickened eyelids of our hills. We were served with food, it was goat meat stew alongside

stiff millet porridge sadza remapfunde. We washed down the delicacies with calabashes filled with traditional mhunga brew both alcoholic (mhamba) and non-alcoholic (maheu) beverages. We ate until our bellies stretched, we couldn't afford a fart or a belch. It was difficult. Dungwiza jumped from his sitting position and an unexpected lightening jolt sparked the semi-dark gallery. It was followed by another unusual lightening wink and a thunder clap. The gallery trembled as if the caves were falling apart. The rainmaker ordered us to be silent and to be stationery. "The gods of this land have heard our concerns, our tears have wetted the mats of heaven, the gods are confirming their love for us and their presence" Dungwiza boasted with his big eyes fixed onto the gallery entrance.

A solitary baboon barked from a distance, a ferocious roar of a lioness ensued, it shook the granite boulders of the shrine and then a strong jolt of lightening blazed again like tongs of fire. There was a deathly silence. We could only hear calculated farts, faint whispers, sighs of awe and feeble breaths from a battalion of congregants packed like sardines against gallery walls. The shrine was seized by the discord of fear.

A frail, thin and uncombed young woman limped lackadaisically into the quite gallery. Dungwiza, Nyamasviswa, shrine desciples and nuns rose in salutation to the unexpected guest amid fish eagle-like cackling ululations, praise incantations and griotic bellows. A song was pod-cracked from amongst the disciples.
It was again a familiar song but many of us were still in utter shock

Tovela, mudzimu dzoka

Ha heyihe mudzimu dzoka

Aee yiye Mudzimu dzoka

Vana Vanogwara mudzimu dzoka

Kwaziwai Tovela

11

It was a song to welcome the spirits of the land.

The frail woman spirit shook her head unstoppably, belched and sneezed incessantly. Her fumbling's were stitched together by continuous handclapping and song

from the shrine disciples. She hung her dreadlocked head languidly twice or thrice and then fumbled for an apparel to cover her beautiful bosom. She sneezed hetsu hestsu hetsu uncontrollably. She roared again like a lioness chasing after a prey. It was an ear-shattering roar. A ferocious roar. She began to speak in a frightening baritone-laced voice. She spoke deep kalanga tongues

"Ndini Tovela

Mutumwa wedenga nepasi

Ndatumwa naMurenga

 Muridzi wapasi nedenga

Chazezesa,

Matama enyu asvika munzeve dzedenga

Ndauya nemisodzi yedenga

Muchamwa mvura, mucharima, muchaguta

Murenga vanotenda nezvipo zvamauya nazvo".

The frail woman spirit was Tovela, the supreme messenger of gods. She was ordained to become supreme when she was still a fetus in her mother's womb. She is the princess of Matonjeni of the patriarch of Murenga Sororenzou. She had brought the message of rain, healing of the land and good life for pilgrims. Tovela Kalanga was the remaining lioness of the holy land. Her service was dipped in sanctity, honesty, dignity and spirituality. A pot of frothing millet beer was offered to her as a gift, she guzzled the beer and blew a wide smile into the awed but obedient congregation. A sign of merriment. We chuckled with the relief that our supplications were received.

Drinking, dance and song persisted. Delinquent disciples imbibed until they crawled like skunks. The sun-rose with its old-aged forehead creased with a paradox of the rainbows and metaphors of rain. Its rays winked to the faint nightly shadows with a calculated rhythm, tearing apart grey and white gowns of mist off our hills. Fingers of dawn caressed the snore-congested gorges and mist-clad mountains of home. Morning doves with their melodious hymns deleted owls all -night poetry slam. The nightly rainmaking ritual and Matonjeni vibe were quickly scribbled onto the godly wind slates.

Tovela and Dungwiza disappeared alongside the grey and white veil of the clearing mist. Song and dance continued. Rains persisted. This is the Mystery of Zame, the holy land of rain, ancestral spirits and gods.

IAM A GRIOT: A Descendant of Rhythm and Ancient Songs

My birth is a metaphor of bullet-traces and the ironic verse
of Leninist style-songs for black liberation that
reverberated the grey mist-clad red mountains of home –
 Zimbabwe.
My birthing was a stitch between the thud of war-time guns
and a heave of pungwe jives. Young women of my
mother's age were volunteer maids during the traumatic but
zeal-oiled Chimurenga times, cooking and washing for the
cadres of liberation. Chimurenga songs sung by these war-
ironed peasant mothers and bullet-toughened collaborators
in the red-hills of Wedza. These Mother-guerrillas endured
the hard throbs of grenades and the thrash of midnight-rains
in those village hills alongside bushy male combatants.
They learnt the soprano of the gun and the tenor of death.
These were heaven-echoing struggle hymns.

On the day of my birth, heavy rains rattled the winter-
crusted red-earth. Rivers sobbed with heaven's tears and

sorrows of war. That gruelling night, swarms of collaborators were moved from one base to another, my earthly goddess was among those pilgrims of war.

...her heartbeat thrilled my tender ears and her blood-ripples lulled my faint soul to sleep. And a stormy foetal spirit rode along with waves of echo and beat of verse. Ingenuity.

I am the blessing of the trip, the child of war song and rain. A mystery.

I am a child of song. I was birthed during the exodus.

That rebel's war was characterized by death, wailing, stampede, bravery, shallow-graves, song and continuous walking. A trailblazing Africa reality show.

My earthly goddess was a dedicated collaborator, volunteer and songstress. She carried freedom in the sacred cave of her womb.

After their strange overnight long walk to freedom base of Mbirashava – rains ceased fire, war-drums paused and their echoes got trapped into the blankets of early day mist. Then came my birth cry they say like an exclamation engraved on the yellow-disc of the smoke-bruised African sun. Claws of dawn caressed the sorrow-soaked red-hills. My goddess wriggled in a thick volcano of red-clay mud, ochre-red blood and dead grass. Her womb groaned from labour pangs and suddenly the wind was cold. June dared the earth and everything in it. Cold-winds whined ferociously to disobedient flora and delinquent vultures. Winter, fast clicking a pause button to the jungle's daily festivals. I was born.

Cadres and collaborators dribbled a liberation jive for my homecoming. They called me Gandanga. I was initiated into this earth by the alto of howling winter-winds, baritones of barking-baboons and the ease soprano of hooting-owls. A child of song.

I was introduced to the festival of sounds, loud and low, good and bad, discordant and beautiful. Upon arriving at the village homestead, the earth trembled, the air got electric with ululations. My paternal grandmother fervently recited a traditional totemic praise poem.

"Chirasha,

 Chikandamina,

Weshanu uri pauta,

 Mavsingo a Govere,

Vari Zimuto,

Mukwasha waMambo,

Vakafura bwe rikabuda ropa"

A lone drum thrilled them into the audience into another dancing routine. The echo of the tinkling drum resonated with the beat of my grandmother's recitations. They said that my eyes winked in response to their merriment. Even up to this day, I beat my chest with pride to that ceremonial reception performed by an elder qualified to be my ancestor.

My old singer-grandmother usually bundled me behind her old but steely back. Lullabies caressed me into dreamland until my goddess returned from her daily errands. I was raised by extraordinary songs, sweet and mellow to every infant's senses.

I enjoyed the ear-tickling ancient poetry. They say I slept to the rhythm of that beautiful lullaby. My grandmother was Gogo in African – she would fall asleep too. Mother returned from the red-clay fields to find us under the watch of spirits and snores.

After some weeks my umbilical cord wilted and fell. They buried it under the hearth near the main fireplace. Thus how we are bonded by our departed clan spirits.

And so I grew up in a highly strict African traditional clan. My father and fellow clansmen brewed ceremonial beer for traditional rites. They supplicated to ancestral gods to end life-tormenting ailments, ravaging hunger, abject poverty and bad omen. Their usual incarnations, totemic praise's performances cultivated the griot in me. Praise and protest poetry became my official language. After my umbilical cord rites, my father gave me a name. He named me after the most powerful battalion of Tshaka Zulu, a battalion that never lost even a single battle – Imbizo. Yes, the names define us and names resonate with our identity. They are strings of belonging.

Time roasted seasons into years. I began drawing meaning from events at home, from school and the village. The throbbing of drums persisted. Traditional ceremonies energized the villages. August was a hive of rituals, in our village Ancestral spirits were raised and cleansing ceremonies were performed. The beat of drums conquered the winds, and their echo was engraved in the chambers of my heart. I rode along with these waves of praise poetry. My father – always dedicated – introduced me to African history, the African kings, the kingdoms, tribes and dialects in Southern Africa. He was passionate about Nguni, about Zulu and Ndebele histories. I was a quick learner and most fascinated by Zulu and Ndebele war cries –

Bathe wena we Zulu,
Senzangakhona KaJama
Tshaka Zulu
Dingane Zulu
Dinizulu
Bayethe ngwalo ngwalo,
Langa
Lemulandulo,

Sombangela,

Mangele Kumalo,

 Ngugulu Kumalo

Bayethe,Bayethe, Bayethe !!!

That mix of African history, the traditional songs,
drumbeats and totemic praises continued to weave a griot
in me.

Zimbabwe attained political freedom in the 1980s. Myself
and other children of war were introduced to the classroom,
the flag and national Anthem. Before Zimbabwe's late poet
laureate Solomon Mutsvairo wrote our own national
anthem, we sang the African Anthem. It was pregnant with
meaning and its rhythm was beautiful.

"Ishe Komberera Africa

 Ngaisimudzire zita rayo

Inzwai miteruro yedu

Nkosi yesikelele Africa..."

Classroom cultivated my literary consciousness. My best
Writer-Poet is Modekai A. Hamutyinei. Most of his poems
were snugged inside the Shona textbook pages for us to

imbibe the rich and deep Karanga verses coated with thought-provoking imagery about identity and morality. His poems christened me into a village griot. My admirers equated my poetry recitations with literary prowess. Our assembly time was electric with poetry recitations. I cherish those childhood moments. I would hurry in front of the whole school with no microphone but armed with a mega phonic voice, Hamutyinei's deep Karanga creamed verses, raw artistic gestures and a confident breath. I exploded verses like a gushing river after a heavy storm.

"Ndainge ndiri ishe zvangu muzvinanyika

Ndirindoga chikara kubva kudoro

Chainge chakandikiya kuti shwe..e

Hwahwa hwamamuchikuye chipanda

Ndaingunotsika matama enzira kudzadzarika,

Svikeyi,mugoto susururu

Rupasa rwangu che-ee

Gumbeze pamusoro wazviona....................."

Hamutyineyi was a great poet of Shona Karanga origin. I

became intimate with his writings. I armed myself with a calabash full of spring-water to wash down the delicacies of his literary showcase into my craving DNA. I sang his verses in pastures and valleys. His verses were heavy with emotion and hefty with affection.

Back into the red-hills after smoking wisdom rolled in book pages. Those red-hills taught me a festival of sounds, beautiful whistles of honey-birds, the pied piping of mother doves, cackling of wild-hens, the baritone of barking-baboons, gushing of rivers, bellowing of bovine of bulls

"A village without sounds lacks rhythm. It is a dead village. A village is a festival of sounds."
punctuated by throbs and thuds of drums echoing from one hill to the other. That festival of sounds serenaded me. A village without sounds lacks rhythm. It is dead village. A village is a festival of sounds.
I want you to know this April is harvesting time.
April is my beloved month with its soul-pricking dew announcing autumn's lost virginity into cough-ridden winter. Earth's green-jacket is suddenly pulled out and replaced by a monkey hat of brown-grass. Bees are happy,

goats are fat, and butterflies are enjoying their last supper as they slowly disappear into the temporary cemetery of seasons.

Fields weep with abundance.

Food is plenty, especially after the rain season's pleasant fart

Villagers thrash sorghum for brew and other rituals. Our household invited the headman and other villagers for a collective thrashing of grain crops. Drums of brew frothed to the brim and the brew was sweet. Calabashes of non-alcoholic millet brew were for non-drinkers. We all salivated from the pleasant smell of goat meat wafting from big pots. Young women and tussling girls scurried in all directions like at a beehive, roasting and making stews. Insults and scorn were thrown to each other amid gulps of sorghum brew. Village delinquents and drinking imbecilic drunks were the centre of attraction. A village stand-up comedy, everyone was equal at such gathering. Humour filled songs were sung one after another. I was raised by this vibe. I loved the rhythm.

"Hoto inorira heya ……..he heya ……..a hoto

Inoririreyi ko?

Cherechedza mukadzi woumwe uchasungwa

Mangwana padare

Cherechedza mukadzi woumwe uchasunga.

Hoto inorira heya…………….he, heya………..a"

Such humorous poetic hymn was magnified into a fat-song and jive. The verses were well-knit to reach the intended audience. Songs were always pregnant with meaning, exposing the rot of adultery and how such sins fail the community. April entertainment was not short of both wisdom and knowledge.

Puberty liberated me and I carried my bag of consciousness, carried totemic praises, drumbeats sound, traditional songs, Zulu war chants and praises … and African history to the city.

A Euphoria of car horns, musical cafes, rowdy and busy streets, political chants, motorcade wails, media wizards, streetwise consciousness further carved my consciousness into reality.

I Am Griot – a descendant of Rhythm and beat of ancient song.

LETTER TO GOD

Somewhere beside Zvagona hills, near Zvamapere 'kopje of hyenas', adjacent to the foothills of Dayataya mountain lies bones and spirits of my great grandfathers and their descendants. I loved this land. Every rainy season, Zvagona hills were village brides fitted in green dresses and floral doek's over their heads. Their lush skin shimmered blue from a distance in the hazy of December sun. Usually, autumn arrived with god's gifts of multi-colored costumes of blooming flowers, their petals nodding erotically to the hesitant sun, the sun winked back secretly to the smiling flowers. Bees and cicadas haunting them like delinquent boys to village damsel's. This time, the earth becomes a beautiful princess scented with natural perfume and clad in floral gowns of pink, yellow, white, peach and ox blood red. June is a vicious dog, it brought howling winds and winter's canines grazed deep into our lives. The earth is undressed into utter nudity. Elephant grass saluted to the passing wind like grandfathers surrendering life. Our hills spotted jailbird's bald shave as they nodded to the winter's sirens: whirlwind and dust ripples. Forests stood shell

26

shocked in their torn overalls. Flowers are tightlipped, their cousins rot into extinction waiting for rain when the earth is born again. The cold bruised sun is a patch on the undergarments of grey horizons. This time, the moon is a hesitant bride. It is winter and nights are ink black and unfriendly. Hyenas wail in pain of winter's bite, regular face-booking of monkeys is on hold. Cicadas are silent like birds. Sometimes hills wept to each other under the veil of mist and the shivering moon lulled our somber souls into sleep until the next morning. When morning comes, the baldheaded hills are ready for a fight, standing proud in anticipation of sunshine or rain, alas the biting winds persisted and the hills are resilient too and similar to the undying spirits of peasants eking out life from tracks of hard red earth on the fringes of Zvagona hills. At night hills were draped in robes of white mist and towards dawn, they fit onto skirts of grey and top gear of blue. We were told ancestors walked alongside the mist at nights and in mornings they would go into deep sleep. The mystery of Zvagona hills, hills of home. During that season, we stacked loads of firewood for warmth, cooking meals and brewing traditional beer. We lived off the forests.

When Gods are angry, the earth is clad in rags like an imbecile. It wears a black torn monkey hat over itself like a pick pocket. The air is taut with foul smell of decaying lives. Baboon's sermons are placed in God's wardrobe. Our creased faces told sorry tales of poverty and hunger gnawing the pits of our bellies

When the red glow of heat persisted like in hell. Silence and barrenness are weaved together onto red earth. While rivers become white washed skeletons of dry sand. Elders spoke in tongues to the wind, we lost their words in the pleats of their elderly language. After some days they traverse to the end of the earth to supplicate Zame, the spirit of rain. Njelele, Zame's disciple would direct them to Nyami Nyami, the goddess of water. They are told to wash their feet and dance to Gods. They were punished for replacing forests with concrete jungles. Birds and spirits of the land were now vagabonds. They are told the earth is simmering in abomination and Gods are angry and choked with carbon laced fumes. They are warned of the coming of devil's triplets: hunger, heat waves and cyclones. They paid their ornaments, applauded the gods and returned to their hovels underneath the fringes of Zvagona hills.

Later, when heavens get overexcited. Gods washed our sins with tears of their joy, rains washed and blessed our land. The earth is born again and is dressed to kill in its usual green gowns and floral doek's. We danced to the clap of thunder and camera flashes of lightening winked at us. Our poverty marinated, yellow maize teeth grinned to sudden glows of lightening. Sometimes lightening jolts sank our tender hearts into our rib -boxes. Zvagona hills also gyrated under the grip of thunder. We danced still for the blessing of rain and rebirth. Our planting fields were patches of alluvial earth between the hems of the hills and the banks of Mamvuramachena "river of white waters". Sooner pumpkins bred like rabbits, veldts wore a silver cap of water and new dark green military combat of sprouting elephant grass. Smells of fresh dung and the scent of fresh udder milk were our morning brew. The new grass fattened our cows, their oily skins shimmered under God's obedient sun.

Our mothers traversed from hill to hill harvesting mushroom, nhedzi, zvihombiro, nzeveyambuya nezhouchuru. Wild mushroom is an African delicacy, a delicacy that raised us from mucus drooling kindergartens into goat bearded grown-ups. Wild fruits of maroro, nhengeni and nhunguru were showered to us by the excited Gods. Bushes became our second homes. We dried fruits and mushroom for the future with the aid of our loving grandmothers. We salivated to the rich fart of roasting meat and baking bread emitted from kitchen huts. Grass beautifies the earth as food beautifies lives. We enjoyed to see our goats getting fat. Bush honey was abundant. We fought successful battles with ferocious red bees for the mouthwatering delicacy, dendende sweet red honey. We accompanied the red honey hunt with a song

Sunga musoro wedendende

Sunga wakanaka dendedende

Sunga musoro wededende,

sunga wakanaka dendende

Sunga wakanaka dendende

sunga wakanaka dendende

The rhythm had returned.

When cockerels announced the new days, eastern hills were beautifully capped with the glow of orange hats from the sparkling sunrays. Baboons cuddled each other in the wake of dawn romance. Rock rabbits jived to the acoustics of cicada tunes and to the discord of village sounds. Mother monkeys rebuked their babies from over eating. Down the stream, fish and toads bathed in smoking falls of fresh water. They are home again. Shezu 'honey bird' spoiled the festival by singing a warning hymn, maybe for another drought to come or death of a reputable person. Nights are stitched with thread of hyena's laughter's and the syntactic hymns of owls.

Our elders sang in contented choruses, nhaka inhara meaning 'the year is blessed with rains'.
We sang to the silver white moon that was fresh from God's mouth as it sat on its throne, over the fontanels of Zvagona hills, Mwedzi wagara ndira uyo tigo tigo ndira – and later with time the moon was ripe to go we bade her farewell mwedzi waora ndira tigo tigo ndira.

Now many years had passed since I left for the city, two decades away from years of dance and abundance. The land is now a wretched vagabond. I am sitting underneath the ragged skirts of mystery hills, pondering if my great ancestor's bones and spirits are still lying here. I see the luxury of rotating seasons is long lost in the abrupt silence of this land. The tenor of birdsongs and baritones of baboons on the mountain zenith is no more. Birds and baboons are long gone, maybe to blessed climes. The joyous scream of hyenas and jackals at dawns was cut short. The joy of reeds dancing to the soprano of mighty streams was remote silenced. A deadly silence.

The sun's heat is menacing as if tongs of red hot charcoal are floating in the air. The heavens are rude and clear blue. Waves of heat turned the earth into a baking oven. Fields are chunks of dried and burnt bread. Trees are strips of roasted biltong. Cyclones passed through and carried away my ancestor's bones to faraway seas. Skeletal dunes of sand replaced our mighty Mamvuramachena 'river of white waters'

Hills are bald headed and wearing a herpes zoster belt around their bellies. They are sweating under the grip of heat caused eczema. I suppose we are cursed. Nyami nyami once warned of hunger, cyclones and heat waves, the menacing triplets.

Behold my earth is naked.

MIDNIGHT CITY

The night is a discord of feverish yearnings from loud vendors, incessant gun claps, and disorderly tenor of car horns. The air is taunted with baritones of groaning old engines coughing their way out of the wincing city. The streets are writhing under the heavy grip of teargas and alcohol laced urine of vagabonds.

Tonight the city is a naked harlot. Its dance is the thud of state police's steely boots in mad run and chase arrests of drug peddlers, sex vendors and forex dealing rascals. Drunk scumbags are wetting street pavements with filthy and snort.

Somewhere closer to an old and dingy police post, a trail of blood led my eyes into the moonlit dingy street. Stray dogs are tearing apart fresh meat from a dumped baby. Maybe the new mother is night crawling in those disease sodden corridor brothels or that she is a trainee recruit of crank-brewing in gutter taverns or the unknown father might be some notorious criminal on police wanted list. Maybe a potbellied fat cat talkative about gender equity and child rights bills in parliamentary sessions. Paradox!

The growls of fighting dogs resonates with rushed groans of masturbating suspects in sordid police cells.
I am watching the night from the roof of an old city brothel.

Downtown under the old bridge, between the bottoms of the frail city. Delinquent boys, serial drunks, life rejects and diehard ex-convicts are sharing a joint under the hesitant wink of the shivering moon.

A battalion.

They are easing their bones after a day's hunt of food in rubbish jungles. Today their dinner is a dozen of expired tins of beef and a crate of burnt bread crumbs.

A lucrative dinner.

They laugh their poverty away between puffs of marijuana and gulps of alleyway brewed crank. Next to their anopheles infested hovel is a narrow stream shitting dysentery and vomiting typhoid. The stream is choked to stagnancy by used condoms, old wigs, decaying bodies and human faeces.
Behind them is an old railway station and a dilapidated

cemetery, usually a haven of wayward cheap sex predators and their raunchy prey.

Every night, the bridge slide into a din of food battles, masturbation groans, mosquito whistles, catfights and lung wrenching influenza.

Sexual groans by morons and drunk harlots add flavor to the daily festival.

The red tin roofed railway station is Satan's pigsty, where the devil reward wayward young lives with the deadly virus, he then release them into the city to spray infections like pesticide. Unknowingly and knowingly many die like sprayed green fleas in trances of midnight excitement.

Mortuaries are harvesting virus - caused deaths every day of God. Sometimes the old bridge battalion spent nights digging up the dead to take away the coffins for resale.

When the battalion is asleep you can hear footsteps of tired snores and drunken dreams floating along with rot of corrupted wind. Delinquent boys hallucinate under the grip of evil spirits. Ex-convicts are haunted by souls of people they killed. You hear them pleading for forgiveness in the depth their nightmares. Cheap harlots supplicate to god to release them from devil's grip. The terminally ill and oldest ones die many times under the attack pediatric and asthma seizures. They are resilient, they rose with the sun like everybody else.

The battalion is mix of small crime and big crime ex - convicts, drug addicts and just wanderers.They are now a tired lot, exhausted by their past and present.

The old bridge is their only home.

A permanent home in summer, winter or rains season.Young sinners prowl the bridge in feverish hunt of food delicacies and good sex, despite the pariah conditions.

The bridge is an export and import station of tuberculosis, dysentery and syphilis. Everyone's penis is rotting from decade long syphilis wounds.

Adjacent to the bridge, just across the railway station life goes on under the veil of frail city lights. Goat bearded maestros, street intellectuals and sloganeering imbeciles' prowl city bars and pimp shabeens. They drown their filthy anger in brown and green bottles. Raunchy dances, raucous laughter's, political gossip and beer are daily lubricants to their heavily depressed mental boxes.

Big fish, well-polished town fellas and important persons come here to spend nights cuddling the bottoms of sex vendors as well as hips of beer mugs. They enjoy their daily toil away from the maddening wives.

Every Friday is a happy day, beer is cheap and sex is free.

The City night club becomes a hive of pole dancing, break dancing, pimping and gambling. The club entry point is characterized by broken sheaths of used condoms, chopped fingers, blood trails, stubbed cigars, torn wigs and many other laughable paraphernalia.

Marriages are made and broken in this den of sins.
Here is where political players deposit the country's future in pink bras. Mugs of cheap whisky castrate city leaders into useless imbeciles. The deadly virus is planted in many lives like maize seed.

At midnight, the city wears its black gown. A lone gutter owl introduces wizards and their cousin sisters into the playground. Illegal vendors invade the streets like ruthless

migrant grasshoppers, Madhumbudya. They pawn
everything from stereos to wedding rings to sugar and
crank.

From where I am sitting right now,
I see the city prostituting our lives and taking bribes.
Corrupt shadows crawling from one street to the other,
hustling for dirty dollars. Alley way sex escapades, blind
couples making kids under the quilt of pavement shadows.
Heartless doctors peddling hospital drugs. Minister's wives
fornicating with bodyguards and garden tenders. Stray dogs
feasting from used and broken condoms. Village mothers
bussed in to sing for an absent president.

The balcony smells of unprotected sex. A viagra peddler is
grinding a pole dancer without a condom and she is
vomiting because of his ruthless pounding. Her snort
perfumes the brothel canteen with a rude smell of cheap
whisky and beef bones. Her vomit also smells like an
expired locally made pesticide, gamatox.
A potbellied anopheles is enjoying Christmas from the
pair's alcohol greased blood. The dancer feverishly winks

to the moon and the frail moon winks back. The drama
continues.....................

Towards dawn the city wears a grey robe in the glow of the
first twilight. The battalion sit around flames of cardboard
boxes made fire. Their limbs are as black as burnt wood in
the first rays of dawn. Their eyes are red like hungry
hyenas. And they are ready to pounce at anything that can
end the war inside their bellies.

As the city yawns out the night's hangover, somewhere
over the bridge, white robbed prophets are bluffing in
tongues and their pilgrims are singing in praise. A
motorcade siren wails loudly and suddenly fades into thin
air. Bus engines puffs their stale fart onto the bridge, the
battalion coughs in a synchronized chorus. Touts are
already in the streets as usual, the city becomes a virgin
again. A cuffed evangelist is pleading to a defiant young
police woman. A swarm of drunken wanderers are pursuing
behind them, chanting vulgar creamed songs. The echo of
their nonsense is drowned by another siren of the new

president's motorcade. It's the 23rd of November 2019. The city throws away the black and grey gowns. It wears a dark green combat and is remote-paused into a presidential minute of silence

PARLIAMENT OF DRUNKARDS

In previous years, the Mandozas hosted the New Years'
parties. They reared sheep and goats, and they invited the
whole village to enjoy roast mutton. There was beer for the
elders, but the young ones were relegated to raspberry and
fizzy beverages. I learned about balloons and tissues at the
Mandoza household. Mandoza himself was once our Father
Christmas, until time burned his years into old age.
But to my surprise, the Mandoza homestead this New Year
was quiet. It was as if somebody had poured a bucket of
ice-water to wet the embers of life in their home. The
silence indicated deep secrets behind those concrete walls.
The magnetic ears of the village had failed to attract any
news from the walled homestead, so no one knew what was
happening.

Despite this, this new year boomed to life with cheap
firecrackers, sparking the heavens open for blessings. The
faint scent of Christmas had vanished, long since fading
into the burning heat. The latest music vibrated the entire
village. We enjoyed so many assorted meats, their tastes

were all as one in our mouths. Fanta and Coca Cola drinks soaked our okra-hardened bellies. We ate English and drank American that day.

Our farting was American. We called it civilized farting.

We hummed Nigerian's P-Square. We imitated and recited Pidgin. We did everything, said everything, and ate everything. We even sighed in Chinese, as Coke fizzled through our black, soot-tamed nostrils. Cousins from Egoli and our capital city had brought niceties. Such was the merriment. Everyone present was high-over-the-hills with excitement.

Yes, our joyful morning went by with its gossip-beat; the afternoon elapsed with sweet odors of roasted meat and sunset shadows, and then, the once-silent Mandoza took over our night by spewing gunshots, death threats, and insults.

Through the roasted-meat-oiled air, the moon peered over our land, and Mandoza's wives–Ndaneta, was leading the

43

pack, followed by Ndagura and a whole swarm of children behind them–dove into our merriment. The fearful intruders sardined themselves into the far end of our packed hut. Mandoza's lips quivered as he glared at them. He refused to blink.

Merry-makers dumped their drinks. The jukebox screeched to silence. Cockroaches scrambled into their closet. Rats followed suit. Children screamed. Dancers packed themselves underneath dinner tables, and some lucky others ducked out behind the hijacker.

Mandoza cuddled his long gun with that devilish grin each of us knew so well. Our murmuring ceased. I heard nothing but the rippling of blood through my heart, although I knew the elders were wishing Mandoza bad omen. Mandoza fired another gunshot, the echo stirring birds from sleep.

The stampede aroused the headman from his sleep. His eyes were blind with sleep and heavy with hangover. He had been dead drunk an hour ago. Now, he lazily scrubbed the sleep off his face. Mandoza was the headman's closest drinking mate. They were as close as dirt-water and fungi.

Mothers clutched their breasts, and young girls winced and wiped their tears with their armpits as Mandoza pointed a gun at the headman, who froze before tottering and falling softly as a cotton ball. Mandoza clobbered Ndaneta with the back of the gun. She barked like a wounded baboon as he crushed his clenched fist into her terrified face. A shower of blood sprayed from her mouth, and she fell–thud. The acrid stink of urine wafted under our noses.

Mandoza shoved his steel gumboot into Ndagura's chest. His daughter waved a thunderous, blinding blow that shook pots and mugs around. It landed on his mouth. He stammered a mouthful of threats. His son gave him another surprising scissors-boot to Mandoza's throat. He lost control, and the gun fell away from him. His eyes drooped, and he stumbled into the silent speakers with a bang.

What happened to cause all this violent commotion? The gossip buzzed around the room. Mandoza's family had refused him to bring his third wife into the homestead. They had boycotted his New Year, his goat and sheep meat. They denied everything from special food to new dresses.

45

He was infuriated and decided to kill all of them.

Now, the headman gained his strength and grabbed the gun from Mandoza's daughter. "Chivara, you want to kill the whole village, vomit your anger?" He dragged him outside for some air.

The headman sent out messengers to bring Jokonia and Jokochwa, the headman's advisers, and the elders would not sleep without answers. The village court gathered with the Mandozas and all interested villagers in attendance. The council of elders sipped from calabashes of sweet frothing brew (it was their custom).

Jokonia was the strictest of headman's advisers, and now, he wiped splashes of sorghum off his mouth with the back of his hands before calling the court to order. He read from the Book of Rules and instructed Mandoza to rise. Mandoza fixed Satan's gaze on him, but Jokonia refused to be cowed. Instead: "Speak! What got into your mind? Speak. The elders want to hear your side. Do not waste our time. The villagers are tired of your games."

"Jokonia I cannot answer anything. You are a tired, corrupt–corr–corrupt–li–lizard." He spat in Jokonia's direction. The court rumbled with reluctant laughter. The headman shook his grey head.

It was now toward midnight. He stood up in haste and waved Ndaneta to stand in the box. She dragged herself from her seat, wiping a rivulet of blood off her face. She made a disturbing loud grunt; she was in deep pain. "Baba want to kill us because we refused his new wife. The new lover is young and is a relative. It's a taboo. Myself and Mainini, we are enough for him." She heaved defiantly. The packed court let out another collective, muffled laugh. Ndaneta sat, wiping away a storm of tears.

Ndagura and the children also testified, and the village women wept bitterly. Mandoza shouted more delusional threats. He cursed his wives' mothers, their cats, their poverty, and their donkeys.

Jokochwa, the self-anointed adviser-in-chief, known confidante of the headman, and staunch drunkard yawned thrice before whispering into the headman's ear. Jokochwa, who drank everything he could get his lips around–crank, malt whiskies, skokian, traditional brew–and had an insatiable craving for meat and cheap gossip, clapped his hands and pulled a cough from the pit of his tobacco-ridden chest. His dirt-coated teeth were only upstaged by his three missing fingers, lost long ago in a robbery tussle.

He stood up to give the final judgment. With a groan, the villagers lost their spirit for a fair call. Jokochwa folded his torn sleeves, as if he wanted to fight; yes, he was good at dampening people's hopes. The headman made a drunken grin before he nodded to signal agreement.

"Mandoza, for disturbing the celebration and wielding a hunting gun, you are charged with breaking the peace of happy villagers. You must pay five bottles of Chateau Brandy, three gallons of skokian, and three goats tonight, now. The council needs to enjoy and celebrate the remain hours of New Year–" Jokowchwa grinned– "and your new bride."

The crowd waited patiently for more in anticipation of further punishment, but to no avail. "Ndaneta, Ndagura, and your puppies, you have two days to pack your belongings and leave the village. We do not keep witches and killers. You can't go against the head of the family. Mandoza has the right to marry more women as long as he wants." He cleared his throat, and with that, the court was adjourned.

Although the grannies of the village beat their chests in disbelief, it came to pass that Mandoza later married his concubine. The village enjoyed meat and beer, and soon after that, he reclaimed the title of Father Christmas.

PROPHETESS

Throbs and thuds of drums tinkered from behind those naked hills. Dogs barked madly as drums continue to tinker from a distance. They continued barking to nothing but rather to the invisible sound of throbbing drums. It was towards the end of winter. Pastures strutted in brown jackets of dead grass. The wind was cold and cheeky baboons yelped in lowered tones. Fields were empty. The night was young and willing to grow. Ambuya Ratsauka was widely awake and mumbling alone in a hushed manner. "He killed you that viper! Dogs are licking bare bottoms of grinding stones. ". Ambuya grunted.

She snorted loudly, black drool splashed from her nostrils. She wept quietly hiding her remorse from the howling winds outside.

"Tisvikewo!" The visitor and his voice were familiar. "Tisvikewo o.......!" The intruder persisted impatiently. Ambuya trotted to the door, wiping the sting of tears with the back of her palms. She heaved an abrupt response with her ever - joyful baritone laced voice. "Ndiani! ndianiko!, aha pindaaa.........i". She enquired, while at same time calculating the shadow of the intruder.

She was surprised to see him visiting her this time of the day. A towering gigantic figure with his handsomeness overshadowed by bushy, cotton tuft hair and neglected grey beard stood by the entrance. He then limped hesitantly into the dark hut. He coughed from the sting of black soot dangling under the thatched roof. His rib shattering cough vibrated the walls. The hut reeked of old stale urine and a strange smell of ancient snuff. The walls were draped in soot coated silver trinkets, tinkling golden coins and smelly rags of goat skin. The visitor pulled his nostrils like a wild baboon.

Amboyna Ratsauka ordered Dandajena to sit more closely since age had burnt her ears.
"Imi chihera. Mutunhu unemhago.Varidzi veDungwiza.Ndati ndikutsikeyi sezvamareva" " Dandajena mumbled a totemic praise before sitting down.He stared fixedly onto Ambuya's

eyeballs. His millet beer scorched mouth trembled. He made a quick gaze outside and then stared back to the motionless bundle of firewood and then back to Ambuya again. Silence interrupted the hot air inside the hut. Ambuya retorted in a frenzy as if possessed, "Don't play with me, sit down.Viper! You soiled the village.Sit down and listen". She jabbed his forehead with her middle finger.Her lips shivered like sunburnt banana leaves. In a jolt of lightening, Ambuya grabbed Dandajena by the torn hem of his ragged overalls. It was a tight bolt grip. She wailed, the echo sent shockwaves into the dilapidating walls. She cornered him the same way boxers do to their opponents.He gasped in utter shock. Ambuya Ratsauka waved a blind fist in his direction. It landed on his face and he spat his front tooth,it was tainted with blood.

Dandajena groaned, bellowed and then tumbled down with a loud thud. She paused a bit thinking that he was dead. She cursed the gods. She rushed towards him and then squatted over his head. She urinated into his right eardrum. Her warm urine smashed him inside. She fanned him with the hems of her torn skirt.He rolled his eyes, an exhibit of being alive. She giggled and spat onto his sweating forehead. Remains of her black drool spattered onto the floor...

Dandajena rose and feverishly squatted near the cold fireplace. He regretted ever coming to her.

"Ambuya I came because you called for me. I will not fight back, the gods will be angry". Dandajena pleaded.

He wiped the sticking remains of the saliva ball on his forehead. Thin layers of blood caked his lips. His upper lip swelled into an ear of wild mushroom.

"Nonsense! They are already angry", Ambuya interjected. He made a high jump stride to the door.

"Dandajena the village is crying, the granaries are yawning with emptiness.
The heavens are laughing at us because of you". She persisted.

She ground her brown teeth and spat harshly into the dying embers of the cold fireplace. An abrupt rush of wind swept across the hut and she giggled again. Dogs barked outside and the wind howled in agreement.

Dandajena scratched his head.

The sound of scratches resonated with the howling winds outside Ambuya's rondavel.

Drums continued to tinker from a distance.

He knelt in front of her, clapping and berating praises. "Ndimi varidzi vepasi. Musaramwa chirongo nokuda kwepwere yenyu. Mhaka inoripwa.Ndipei mukana. Shava yangu nhuka." He recited the praise with his heart stuck in the throat.

Sounds of the barking dogs slowly faded and got succeeded by midnight cockerel alarms from beyond those grey hills. Dandajena village had lost its usual rhythm due to incessant droughts. No more bird songs, riverside gossips, cockerel alarms or barking dogs. The vibe was long gone. Planting fields remained fallow for years. Naked skies hesitantly winked to the bare bottoms of the village.Danda hills stood confidently in their bald shave, suffering the humiliation of the roasting hell of a sun. Incessant droughts rendered the village lifeless. The air was hot and thick with rot. The stench of dying and dead lives choked the breath of that earth. Elders sold off their daughters for food rations.

Barter trade.

The alarming cockerels helped to ease the drama inside the hut.

A pot of millet beer stood there in a lone stature. It frothed to the brim like the smile of a full moon. It was emitting a sweet and beautiful scent of freshly baked bread. The catchy smell wafted around the hut.

Dandajena snorted carelessly.
He salivated and wetted his cracking lips with his tongue. Ambuya staggered from the trap of her slumber as if seized by demons. She lifted the pot of brew with a whirlwind grip. She made loud swigs and her gulps were heavy..She stole a rushed glance outside and then shoved a cup of millet brew into Dandajena's hands. He cracked a wide smile for the first time that night. He swigged madly.

Afterwards, she summoned Dandajena to carry her drum. She carried a pot of brew over her cotton tuft head.

Ambuya was beautiful.

She had a serrated tooth and her waist beards were made of wild seeds. Their jingling sounds resonated with her gigantic strides towards the river. She was leading the way. She fumbled a song until they arrived. It was an ancient traditional hymn. It was their traditional hymn. The lines were difficult to master. Ambuya warned him not to say any word unless she ordered him to.

Dandajena nodded in agreement.
The scent of rotting carcasses crept around the river. A clatter of whitewashed bones covered up for that sorry state. The midnight air was tense and demonic.
Ambuya bellowed and belched incessantly.

They knelt down beside the dark enclosure of river made of rock boulders. Ambuya Ratsauka poured three gulps of millet beer on mounds of sand and sniffed from the snuff container made from ram's horn. That horn was her souvenir. She sneezed unstoppably amid silent whispers and hushed incantations. She bellowed again from the pit of her belly, pleading with the blowing winds, the air, the spirits and the god's for forgiveness.

Ambuya instructed Dandajena to imitate after her. They clapped their hands with a supplicating thud, facing the balding hills of home.

She fumbled some poetic verses,
"Kunemwi varidzi vemvura.

Vanoinaisa nokupfekedza nyika

.Ndauya nayo ndumure iye kuzoreva mhosva.

Botso tariona tapfidza.

Tipeiwo donhodzo vazukuru vagute.

Imwi varipasi.

Varikumhepo.

Nemwi Nyadenga,

Musikavanhu noMupi wazvose."
Ambuya Ratsauka wept bitterly, her trembling forefinger

pointed to the direction of the decaying village.

A gust of invisible wind swept through her eyes to nowhere. A fat bead of tears drenched her dust clutched feet. She ordered Dandajena to beat the drum slowly. She mumbled a hymn under her lips.It grew into a fatty ancestral song. It popcorn - cracked into the thickness of the night.She trotted back and forth as the drum tinkled in agreement with her dance steps.She slid into another spirited frenzy. Her gourd shaped head shook languidly in an unstoppable trail of trances. She sprinkled a shower of black snuff into the wind, blowing it to all directions of the earth.Storms of sweat poured over her old but delicate frame. Lightening flashed in a wink of a second.It cracked with a heart- thudding jolt.

Dandajena was left dazed as Ambuya disappeared alongside the lightening thread. Fear seized his heart and a shower of sweat trickled down his age smitten spine.

Ambuya returned abruptly than his expectation. Her right hand was tightly holding a mound of fresh mud. Dandajena's mouth gaped in awe.He wanted to speak, he then reminded himself of the previous warning.Darkness soon blanketed the earth. Heavy clouds billowed above lazy and tired hills of the east. Spiritual quietness replaced the village's deathly silence. Thunder roared, flashes of lightening streaked across the drought shaved pastures. A heavy down pour cleansed the abominated village.

Ambuya smiled as heaven's tears washed away sins from the land of her fathers. Frogs, fervent patriots of rain giggled with joy in sheets of floating water. Dawn arrived as if nothing had happened. It carried bold rays of hope that erased the tight grip of darkness from the land, the sun as though a yellow ball peeped through the newly rain washed hills.Its rays passionately caressing the tired skin of those village elders.

"Dandajena! Dandajena! Dandajena!

Do not kill the Nyami Nyami again". Ambuya was choked by her last words.

Tears bathed Dandajena's old beard. He wobbled towards home like a squashed worm. Ironically damp air around was pleasant and new. He drank gulps of that refreshment with mixed feelings of content and sudden loss. He sobbed profusely for Ambuya's sudden death.

PRINCE OF SATAN

A solitary baboon barked throughout the night. The barking sound was the stitch between silence and darkness. Dogs never barked to anything. Owls were ironically trapped in their dark nests. Dawn arrived unexpectedly.

My father coughed from the pit of his lungs.My skin tightened because his cough was deep. His incessant loud snores disturbed the silence. Fingers of the sun soon filtered into my torn blanket. Intense heat pricked my whip lashed back.I felt an irritating pain inside me.

I sneaked out of my night trap with a bold start and peeped into the real world through the crevices of my rondavel.

I couldn't believe my innocent eyes, just outside next to river, stray dogs whined and snarled amid a leisurely sexual act. I made an embarrassed laughter. They danced in their act as if seized by epilepsy seizures. Their madly love making howls attracted the attention of some errand dogs appearing from behind the nearby bushes in rushed hunt of rodents.

The vicious bull dogs snarled to scare the male partner on top. It ran away tuning a cowardice whine, leaving its sex partner in the shame of other dogs. The remaining partner got mad like a wounded lioness. It fought the attackers of her mate to the victorious end. Dust enveloped the scene as bulldogs howled haplessly under the fierce attack of the bitch. They surrendered in blinded directions.

Machena remained at the drama scene snarling with the air of defeat.I pelted it with a stone. It ran away faster than a wind ripple. It howled still in defiance and then melted into the hazy of the shimmering December heat. I spat a goblet of anger into the burning dust. I crushed it under my cracked feet.

"Dogs are always dogs". I cursed the creator for once in my lifetime. The morning ballooned into a filled day.

The air was pregnant with heat.

Beads of sweat splashed all over my body. The sky was in its usual bald shave. The earth was silent as if everyone had been summoned to hell. May be God wanted to announce the proverbial end of the world. Hell had paid us homage.Triplets hunger, drought and poverty roasted us into biltong. Dying and living were now the same. The river was fast dwindling. Gossip remained the source of life.The rumor of mermaids soon faded into oblivion. Crocodiles disappeared into their caves without any visible trace.Time ticked away as hours were fattened into days by each minute.

 I was unexpectedly startled by an abrupt, rib crushing wail. It was as if a jolt of lightening had ripped through my heart. I hesitated on my sit and nearly wetted my pants. The wail echoed again, arousing tiny insects to life.The persisting cries brought the once silent village to a jostling and stampeding theatre fiesta. My stomach twisted. My heart drummed inside my chest box.

My blood rushed.

I rushed outside to wedge my thin self into thickness of raging crowd.

A beehive crowd swarmed around Bvambu's rondavel. Some nodded with distress and some yelped in trances of anger.Confusion was written all over their awe- creased faces. Many watched the unfolding drama in utter astonishment.The river gushed heavily in response to the villagers mood.

I was clueless and stone shocked.

My father was inside the maddening crowd. Bvambu was standing there stark naked, wincing in pain, covering the part between his legs with bloody hands.A random splash of condensed milk semen sat ugly on his right thigh. He was bleeding profusely. The glint of life was fast fading off his eyes,

That days experience bleached him into a mound of pale white clay. Bvambu was known for his hunting prowess, many called prince of the forest. That day he missed a good catch. He caught a wrong one. He failed to skin the wrong catch alive this time around.

To my teeth gritting amazement, Runako coughed out and spat Bvambu foreskin onto the dust. She crushed it with edified vehemence. Her round lips quivered with grief.Grannies were dazed.Many were tongue tied. Bvambu remained hapless. His gigantic figure was reduced to a rock lizard by a village girl. She ripped off his foreskin from his entire penis in a tussle to defend herself.

 She unapologetically lifted his torn underpants in the air to the full glare of the whole village. A gust of wind rustled through carrying the untraceable bouts of laughter from hesitant voices in the crowd.My tongue dried in my mouth.I sneezed to avoid further embarrassment.Bvambu exhibited an abrupt devilish grin of shame.He cast a long i stare towards Runako's direction as if he wanted to swallow her.

"Bvambu grabbed me from the river Tugwe.

 I was taking a quick bath.

He crushed my breasts and pruned me naked to….. and forced me to suck his………." She stammered and failed to complete the last blurb. There was a rushed murmur from crowd, a retreat and then a stampede as women pelted heavy stones and brooms towards Bvambu.

64

Marunjeya Runako's mother grabbed Bvambu by his throat. He gulped cups of forced air. He made a loud fart. His lungs choked and they rolled down together for several minutes. Gasps of their battles filled the rondavel. Bvambu lost his finger in the battle.

Runako's mother fainted instantly.

"He said he wanted to give me roasted meat, as my belated Christmas present. I refused and he closed my mouth. I clutched the pipe of his male gun and crushed". Runako persisted,she sobbed profusely as the drool of fear splashed her bare breasts. I felt a rushed fever in my spine as they quivered like unattended ripe mangoes. I was not alone.

A great applause thundered from irate villagers. Insults and pebbles rained into Bvambu's face. The headman whisked him to Runde Clinic.

Villagers scattered back to their lone homesteads. Runako had a tender peach skin with chocolate brown lips that cracked a seductive, convincing cherry plum smile.

65

She carried breasts worth a fortune of precious gold.. Soft words fell from her mouth like mountain drizzle. Her figure resembled a bundle of diamond beads.Her looks were bold and her guinea pea eyes, a gift of stars Runako was an amazing craft that God has given his whole time, talent and creativity. My mother cherished her beauty.

Runako had refused the prince of Satan to contaminate her dignity for an ounce of roasted meat. Her fame lingered in our village and others for many years.

The drama didn't end but paused. Bvambu strangled himself with a bandage in a hospital apartment. News of his death wafted into the entire village like the scent of newly baked bread.

He was later unceremoniously laid to rest by seven elders far away from the village rhythm, inside the hills of grey mist. Elders advised that suicide deaths were not to be mourned in homesteads.

Such abominations would birth into evils of hunger and unending droughts. Runako later travelled to the big city to further her studies.

DIMPLES OF FREEDOM

Dimples of mighty river donga, river
Sokoto flowing honey of liberation, dripping sweetness of
decades

Of freedom harvest

Taraba and ekuku flowing with seasons coming after one
another

Winters in tears and summers in blood

Dimples of freedom sing freedom
Freedom of the people, people and their song

The resonance of rhythm, rhythm of drumbeat throbbing

Tsaunin mainono, veins of tsaunin Kure, throbbing the
heart of tsaunin ukuru

Rhythm throbbing under the feet of mothers and children
pounding this earth sodden in oil and hope.
Dimples of freedom
You age with generations like baobab

The essence of villages and the resonance of tribes

Tribes singing embracing the dimples of silver moon

Singing one tune, in one tongue, sing boki mothers, rise mbumbe sisters

Sing bachere songs, dance the gavako dance

Dimples of freedom

You age with generations like banana trees

Kings of this land, i sing of you

My song of bones, shadows, stones, mist and smoke

Dimples of freedom

I sing of kings whose skin glow after the caress of coco butter

Their breath smelling the milk of coconut

I sing with modibo of gombe, obong of obioko, olu of Warri

I sing of you baban lamido, oba of Lagos

Dimples of freedom smile with olo of the olowo

Dimples of freedom
Smelling decades of light and stink

Enduring decades of nights and hope

Sleeping in decades of nightmares and dreams

Rivers gobe, ekulu and aba, rise for freedom

Your stomachs vomiting the sun of liberation, liberation

That crocodiles and reptiles be pregnant with the sun of
liberation and

The moon of freedom

Dimples of freedom
On top of tsaunin kuki, tasunin shamaimba, doves and owls
hooting

And cooing the dark of nights and newness of mornings

Dimples of freedom smile to the mountains of this land

This is my poetic grapefruit to the land that breakfasted

Omelets of bitterness and beetroot of sweetness

Dimples of freedom
This is my succulent watermelon of metaphors to the land
whose is heart is

Velvet and whose soul is a grain of wheat

Dimples of freedom sing with me, the song of freedom,

Sing Bello, sing azikiwe, sing awolowo, and sing shehu

Song of the people, people and their song.

IDENTITY APPLES

I am a fat skeleton, resurrecting

from the sad memories of dada

and dark mysteries of animism

I am Buganda

I bleed hope

I drip the honey of fortune

Makerere; think tank of Africa

I dance with you wakimbizi dance

I am Tanganyika

I smell and fester with the smoke of African genesis

I am the beginning

Kilimanjaro; the anthill of rituals

I am the smile of Africa

My glee erase the deception of sadness

my tooth bling freedom

I am myself, I am Gambia

When others sleep with bullets stuck in their stomachs

I sneeze copper spoons from my mouth every dawn

I am the Colombia of Africa

I am the Cinderella of Africa

where mediums feast with the ghost of Kamuzu in Mulange

trees

Here spirits walk naked and free

I am the land of sensations

I am the land of reactions

Coughing forex blues

Squander mania

I still smell the scent of Nehanda's breath

I am African renaissance blooming

I stink the soot of Chimurenga

I am the mute laughter of Njelele hills

I am Soweto

Swallowed by Kwaito and gong

I am a decade of wrong and gong

I am the blister of freedom vomited from the belly of

apartheid

I see the dawn of the coming sun in Madiba's eyebrows

I am Abuja

Blast furnace of corruption

Nigeria, the Jerusalem of noblemen, priests, professors and
prophets

I am Guinea, i bling with African ;floridization'

I am blessed with many tongues
My thighs washed by river Nile
I am the mystery of pyramids
I am the graffiti of Nefertiti
I am the rich breast of Nzinga

I am Switzerland of Africa
The rhythm of Kalahari sunset
the rhyme of Sahara, yapping, yelping
I am Damara, I am Herero, I am Nama, I am lozi, and I am
Vambo

I am bitterness, I am sweetness
I am Liberia

I am king kongo
Mobutu roasted my diamonds into the stink of deep brown
blisters
Frying daughters in corruption microwaves

Souls swallowed by the beat of Ndombolo and the wind of
Rhumba
I am the Paris of Africa
I see my wounds
I am rhythm of beauty
I am Congo
I am Bantu
I am Jola
I am Mandinga

I sing of you
I sing Thixo
I sing of Ogun
I sing of God
I sing of Tshaka
I sing of Jesus

I sing of children
of Garangaja and Banyamulenge
whose sun is dozing in the mist of poverty
I am the ghost of Mombasa
I am the virginity of Nyanza

74

I am scarlet face of Mandingo
I am cherry lips of Buganda

Come Sankara, come Wagadugu
I am Msiri of Garangadze kingdom

My heart beats under rhythm of words and dance
I am the dead in the trees blowing with wind,
I cannot be deleted by civilization.
I am not Kaffir, I am not Khoisan

I am the sun breaking from the villages of the east with
great inspiration of revolutions
its fingers caressing the bloom of hibiscus

Liberation!

Iron Wind

(Hybrid Essay)

The world has known divisions for as long as history can
remember. From
strength that overrides others to the weakness that attracts
marauding gangs
of men of ambition and cunning. Adventure has led some
into what they
termed "discoveries" of Rivers and their sources, of
Mountains high and
majestic, and a people so different in their cultural
environments, that to
the eye of a visitor, they appeared other worldly.
The world has never run short of divisive tools and terms to
keep one for
each. From the irony of heights and weights, to the
delight's and
indecency of dark humor based on foods and drinks and a
people's culture.

GOD and god's have their roles and stamps on a people's interpretations,

raging from waging wars to convert and dominate, to whole sale massacres

because others beliefs were less acceptable to a deity followed by a

muscular power. In the name of many known Faiths, man has suffered

immensely and continue to suffer even under the full glare of a world that

is so connected, that nothing escapes the owl eyed social Media/internet

never sleeping eyes.

If it's not belief it's something else that pits one man to another. Color

has played the worst card in segregation of humanity. Regimes are known to

have come up with a cultic panacea of annihilating all who were less than

their proscribed hue, height and eye color in a so called super race.

Commerce has not particularly done well to hide i's dismal take on the
lesser endowed in terms of what the world considers
GDP....Countries are graded into first, second and third
world. Countries comprise individual
human beings. Once categorized in numerical terms, they cease to have a
human quality and adopt a statistical stature.

Dehumanizing poverty by demonizing it and those suffering
the "pauper malady". Terms like " those who survive under
a dollar a day. A people labelled by lack. Another labelled
by luck.

Divisions.
Then came weaponry and sophistication. Guns and canned
Carnage. Bombs as heroism spoke to the Sky over
Nagasaki and Hiroshima. More divisions follow. Giants
with cold threats lying under silos of frozen homes
awaiting disagreements. What a time of it the world had!
But like all eras, this too came to an end with trumpets of

fragmentation scattering the deadly

embers of stored caches of annihilation finding its ways into eager

markets of rogue juvenile quarters ready to tussle for positions of

"global respect" through "fire power"

Ideology made no sense. Religion was cowed. No one was immune to the future

that loomed on the human collective heads as each goon state thumped it's

nukes chest.

How times change!

A new baby was born in the East. A baby with an attitude like a thief.

Escaping its parents unloving gloved hands, it flew first into the neighborhood, dropping its ghastly faces on the heads of its makers kin.

Death. Sinister death. The wind took the 'birdlings' over the border, across

the oceans on the comforts of cruise ships. And luxury

living became a

nightmare. Right now, quarantine is not for rabid dogs or
lepers in their

colonies.

It's what no longer divides that divides us. What irony! We
are faced by an

enemy of our own intellect taken over conscious. Our own
intelligence

exceeding common sense. Our own genius gone insane.

In it all, regardless of mitigation measures, one thing
speaks a human

language. It's no longer about class, color or Creed. it's not
even about

ideology or theology. It's about being careful to survive the
monster we

have made. And the world suddenly speaks "humanese"

How I wish we didn't have to face such an ugly and tragic

catastrophe to bring us to the realization of the folly of

excessive greed in pursuit ofglory and power over others.

If we survive, we may have to analyze our engagement

with dark matters that that put life at risk. If we don't, we are to blame for our end.

For now, let's keep hygienic, keep to ourselves, bury our Dead, care for the

dying and think of how we have arrived at where we are.

While at it, let's pray. For regardless of our form of worship, days of

worship, mode of worship and the dress code in worship, we all pray to a

Higher power. He may yet hear our prayers and led a hand.

YOU SEE, praying is personal and communal if you will. Worship places are

closing fast, if not faster than bars and deli's. Offices are closing fast,

if not faster than schools.

Only true saints are at work. Those medics and their assistants and the guys who must fill the supermarket shelves with your basics.If you ask me, the very deity we seek in those buildings, is inside us andthose selfless humans who take chances with their lives to take charge of ours. They are the ones mellowing down the iron wind of a viral onslaught on humanity right now.

MISSED MOMENT, MIND BUMPS AND LOCKED PADDOCKS

It's based on my experiences during COVID 19
Lockdowns as an exiled Poet living in a foreign country*

Calling the morning with a mournful urgency, sleep fell off
the
routine checks of protocol and the gong silently, if
urgently,
summoned a sermon of fleeting feet. A son beheld the
sun's shadow with
loving thoughts packed hurriedly into a strained back. The
beauty of
smooth roads and distance hills failed dismally to tell the
dreams on
a runway refusing crafts to land. Temporariness is a weed
with long
tendrils as only those with healthy respect for shadows
know. To part
with tomorrow's hope to the hands of a paid Piper whose
mission in "

82

his appointed career" is to poach livelihoods of passerby's in quest

for a night's nest on this migratory routine is a pain bordering on a

tooth extraction without anesthesia. That this accepted sin is

described in business lingo as lucrative is tearing off fresh from the

living and asking to be thanked.

And the revolutionary chant is not over!!!

Am blind and love it because that way I judge nobody.

Am deaf and trust it because that way I hear only hope from Angels from a far.

Am immune to cold and heat so the elements don't scare me,

I am a lamp post planted by hands I can only guess at. Am a child and

a man honest enough to acknowledge God exists in the spirit of

creation and the heart of men however few.

When boarders slam doors louder than an irate spouse demonstrating

disgust at an assumed slight by love, common sense stirs the soul for

an instinctive triple jump.

Am a son of the South where the sun rises with the song of the hills

and cattle calling milk to duty,

Milk is a source of life and it's absence is a bitter song that speaks

kwashiorkor and other third rate needs unmet.

Am a product of great souls that the universe unites to clear the

morning smog with a hearts torch.

And the struggle song is not over!!!

What is Man but a product of Man?

I refuse to reject humanity and I do it with humility.

Where I am is a location whose dust reminds me of my earliest form and

my final formlessness.

I am a journey on a travel and now is time to chant an old
tune,
That no struggle is without cause and course if it's the one
that chose you,
And in the beauty of such times as we are living in, islands
within,
Am counting thousands of breaths in gratitude for the spice
that life
and living is.
For spice true, is in the variety,
Not only of terrain but of origin,
But also the hand that tended it,
The hand that picked and packed it,
As such,
Making the whole a part of the bits and vice versa.
Cycles refuse to rest, like a month in flight, a soul flies in
the
night leaving a sad dream on a prodigal sons wet eyelids,
And the liberation vibe is not far,
Who can say the taste of life is anything but mysterious and
hard at it's best?

News is best at its absence if it's not the birth of a child,

Am awake to all truths even the most banal and morbid,

Am human enough to weep at wickedness and laugh at jest,

But tell me fair men of this land that " unlanded" me how to virtually

bury my own,

Tell me like am a three year old how to grieve with dignity this

vehicle that bore me to your shores and must now bid a silent goodbye

in my blinded monastery upon this cavernous existence,

And the redemption thunder is rumbling more closer!!!

Am flesh and flesh has demands to weep and touch its own in making

and unmaking,

Who will roll this mist back a day and allow a wish to plan a shared hug?

Am a child of the universe bleeding hard on the winds that make

commandments of demented buffoonery,

I fall on these weakened knees sending this mute anguish
up into the bloated clouds,
If I see tomorrow it's all because silence has given me a
route to
walk in this barren vacuum of misplaced hunger of human
touch,
That voices sprout hands that feed my sanity with a purity
only angels know, am grateful,
And some day, when the grass has grown over that mound
that settled unto itself,
This boy with a grey beard shall come back to plant a fruit
tree on
the home square and name it " Silver" in honor of all dawns
and dusks,
And the tender hands that give me dew upon this journey at
the earliest of arrivals.
Am all that because you are all that, even as you now ride
the stars
in the silence of night and the wind of days.
And the revolutionary chanters are chanting still
It's not yet uhuru, Aluta Continua, the fight and chant for
freedom Continues.

THE ROAD TO ZVEGONA

Is fading the memory of its son,

Who for words must ride the night

Fleeing ears that hear thunder on a baby's purity gaggle,

Zvegona, my homestead,

Ancestors are watching

Elders on a scheming mission

Trading lies with more lies

The road to Zvegona

Your Sideroads sigh

Your song is silent

Only hiccups of mothers greet the sun

Yearning for the return of the bearded child

Who lives on the strings of truth

Truth refused a seat at the council of baboons on the lagoons

Goons settling scores on the assumptions that a boy has a
price,

Well, the boy true has a price

But not one you can pay with looted coins

The boy has shaved his hair not his brains

The boy has slipped his boots on and truth has raised its
flag

And the spirits of truth sing his Achilles heels on,

So Zvegona, the village of the lucky poet,

Grow thistles and thorns

Feed cattle and goats

The boy has shaved his beard

Ready for a walk back, to shave the land of all pretentious
shenanigans

Uprooting the weeds and weevils

Repair the kraal too,

Where roosters shall announce light unto the land,

Currently bent double under the gargantuan weight of lying tongues.

Zvegona, you are my yesterday

Zvegona, you are my tomorrow in whatever form, shape or

. . . .

MAPUNGUBWE

Land of baobab, land of eagles

Mapungubwe,sagging with ambition of nujoma,madikizela
and sobukwe

Land of crocodiles and spiritual eagles- Mapungubwe

Rivers groaning with sweet tongues and sacred laughter

Mapungubwe – dream of stones

Bones and spirits quietly sleeping under the burden of
peaceful rocks

Your songs, mapungubwe rhythm to bones of dead heroes
and sleeping heroines

Mapungubwe,crying tears of laughter, struggle and
freedom,

 Mapungubwe!

DREAMS OF MY ANCESTOR

a dedication to my mother

(i)

Our village rondavels sat on the peripheral fringes of
Dayataya,

Dayataya, the elephantine mountain of home.

It cracks a fervent babyish glee every dawn.

I enjoyed the beauty of mist that lingers onto its forehead
every night fall.

Birds sang incessantly as if answering back to the echoes
of ever- yelping baboons.

Monkeys face –booking onto tree –branches, enjoying the
glee of every new day

Rock rabbits jiving diligently to the discord of laughing
hyenas

As wild hens quacked in their gossiping tenor

In synch to the soprano of ever-gushing streams.

Mothers armed with peasantry zeal

And stereotyping loyalty to their matrimonial religions

Thrashing and grinding millet in wood mortars,

The aftermath is the brewing of a delicacy,

A beloved village beverage,

traditional millet beer(Ndari) or (mhamba).
scumbags drank the brew to the dregs,

Their stupor oiled hymns were succulent with rhythm

And turgid with reason.

(ii)
I sang along with the village rhythm,

the chirruping of small birds over soot- clad rondavels,

The alto of doves as they triumphantly imitate angels of
dawn towards dawn

The trotting footsteps of the sun as gigantic rays walk over the creased mats of horizons

in their triumphant march to the promise of midday.

I cherished those mountains, when dressed in grey gowns of mist

And awed by pastures donning the heavy green military combat,

the baritone concocted sounds of barking baboons

above the fontanel of red hills of home,

The beat of rain and the echo of thunderclaps,

The stitch of lightning bolts onto the gyrating earth,

Stitching together valleys and mountains on the pleats of heavens

I loved the smell of fresh cow under milk concocted with fresh steaming cow dung,

The scent of fresh mud after a thorough whipping of the earth by incessant downpours

(iii)

Dayataya worn a light-yellow tinge on its head at dawn.

Toward sunset it cracked a harmless red ox-blood tinted smile.

Dayataya,the elephantine mountain of home.

 Its cousin, Zvegona, remained holy and steadfast,

Enduring whipping seasons of droughts and winters.

it never surrenders to ravaging hurricanes and tumultuous cyclones.

 Zvegona strutted in grey gowns during winter mornings.

At night, it switched to black to match with its distant cousin, Dayataya

 Dayataya lulled us to sleep and guided us from bad omens.

And at that time Corona Virus

And his ancestor, Influenza

 And his medium spirit,Whooping cough were not yet born,

The earth was once a virgin and holy as a country damsel.

When, Zvamapere hills danced in blue bridal veils towards sunset

Gwenyuchi strutted in grey suit of the clearing mist

When Gwenyuchi passes the holy mist to beloved Zvegona through an emotionally kiss

We all giggled with joy at nature's lovely escapades.

And when hunger folded its legs on our doorsteps
As our stomachs run battles with emptiness,

Mama Godess of all times

You persisted and won battles against hunger.

When poverty erected its manhood into our homestead,

You fumbled metaphors to gods and you chanted resistance.

Then poverty, the coward scampered to other villages,

.(iiiii)

I am child of war,
 of rain and road

 A child of freedom songs.

I smelt the rhythm of Chimurenga

And the wave of gun smoke.

 As I dangled on your struggle - hardened back,

 I carved poetry from your sweet lullabies
And grieving hymns,

 I became a griot before I teethed.

, I am a griot of the land.

I speak to Kings and Queens,

I sing verses for mediums and revolutionaries.

 You remain my goddess of all times.

On the day of my birthing

the moon was torn into two halves,

Wind raged,

A storm ensued,

Thunder clapped the red earth,

Lightning bolts cracked in synchrony with gun claps.

The rat tat of pelting raindrops witnessed your labor pains
on God's night.

 I was born.

Freedom songs re- vibrated our grenade scorched earth

peasants of red hills danced fervently to my revolutionary

birthing

My tender soul smiled at the paradox.

 Father named me, Gandanga reChimurenga

Father had imbibed the socialist revolutionary propaganda

whisky,

That castrated his psyche to worship ideological black
cockerels

Father munched the Nkurumaist-Castroist-Mugabeist
freedom biscuits

Patronized ......

Nevertheless, today black cockerels drink the revolutionary eggs

Their tyrant imbeciles imbibed the liberation milk,

We remained holding to title-deeds of poverty dressed in torn rags of the struggle

Sidelined ......

And later after the song and dance,

 You returned to scratch for dear life on the rocky fringes of Dayataya

The elephantine mountain of home

Dayataya, the distant of cousin of Zvegona hills

And ancestor of Mbirashava, the redhills of home

Still, you remained the goddess of all times.
Time passed and the gods and ancestors freed me from the bondage of Satan.

 I grew perfectly then like a sweet potato enjoying the caress of red earth.

Years stewed into decades and decades fried themselves
into more decades.

(iiiiii)

In the wake of a pregnant anopheles [a type of mosquito]

  humming its blood-sucking hymn,

  and after bedbugs launched a terrorist bombing against my
skin,

  I got dizzy and convulsed.

  I swatted the mosquitos with my big thumb

and the bedbugs scattered in no time.

I dreamt of you Mother, wearing a sparkling silver wedding
dress,
walking side by side by the great king of all times,
  my departed father. I carried a lit white candle
and you had a bunch of white roses.

A wedding song boomed feverishly
from a big stereo.

I can't remember the singer, but I remember the beautiful
poetic song,

Vul'indlela wemamgobhozi
He unyana wam
Helele uyashada namhlanje

iiiiiii)
Time fried years into decades

I learnt the language of hustle and bustle in the city of no
sleep.

I stumbled upon hermits vomiting the snort of illicit beer

 Harlots in their mad-run chasing potbellied sex imbeciles
in darkest thickets of nights,
fake prophets double –dipping and molesting their miracle
hungry clue-less congregants.
 Cheap ropaganda songs cascading from hovels of
congested suburbs
Here voters breakfast on stale bread and cheap crank.
Cousin sisters and sisters pimping their dignity for political
doeks

Streets wincing from slogan chants, teargas, gun claps and gutter-slang

iiiiiiiii)
The revolution is roasting its own daughters for supper.

The devil birthed a cruel goblin of a son called Corona Virus.

every door of every home is locked.

Every gate of every country is locked.

Goddess, I was not there to cast the last lump of shovel dust,
to say goodbye spirit Queen

I failed to weep not because I am a coward.

Today as I write this eulogy and my heart- caves bleed with grief
I remain chanting resilience as every morning I see you floating in the mist of dawn
and later wrapped in the cloaked night of harmony

Fambai Zvakanaka Shoko

Makwiramiti, mahomu-homu

Vanopona nekuba

Vanamushamba negore

Makumbo mana muswe weshanu

Hekani Soko yangu yiyi

Vakaera mutupo umwe nashe

Vana Va Pfumojena

Vakabva Guruuswa

Soko Mbire ya Svosve

Vanobva Hwedza

Vapfuri vemhangura

Veku Matonjeni vanaisi vemvura

Zvaitwa matarira vari mumabwe

Mhanimani tonodya, svosve tichobovera

Maita zvenyu rudzi rukuru

Matangakugara

Vakawana ushe neuchenjeri

Vakufamba hujeukidza kwandabva

Pagerwe rinongova jemedzanwa

Kugara hukwenya-kwenya

Vari mawere maramba kurimba

Vamazvikongonyadza kufamba hukanya

Zvibwezvitedza, zvinotedzera vari kure

Asi vari padyo vachitamba nazvo

Zvaitwa mukanya rudzi rusina chiramwa

Maita vari Makoromokwa, Mugarandaguta

Aiwa zvaonekwa Vhudzijena

You remain the goddess of all times.

I chant resilience!

ALONG THE WRETCHED ROAD

Immersed in the cauldron of swirling floods, I flap my
weighted wings with a singular drive carrying my dreams
in a perforated duffle bag. My feet seek the sun at midnight
in the land processing its abortion of tomorrow under the
snipers telescope so no truth escapes unpunished. I am a
child of the South thrown further South where oceans crash
with the fury of disagreed temperament. I am the child of
the red soil darkened by falsehoods of high priests reading
marching orders of disorders from a dishonored group
purporting to speak for gods of democracy.
North is more than a direction as my eternal campus throbs
against the steel fetters of burnt hope as the night lights a
path to the horizon dragging the flag of my totem along
strangers homesteads.

Baptized again and again by black night by men with no
names, I now acquire a new name and a newer status. They
baptized me grasshopper and I had to agree. Being a long
jumper, being a high jumper and now attempting the triple

jump, grasshopper sounded a fair baptism name for a
newborn boy man lost the long road to the finish line under
chase of fathers without hearts. The process demanded

I hit the road twice as hard into the no man's square where
mutation is official identity and 'refugeeism' an
international tag that comes in handy in the categorization
of run-away undesirables as State gossip has branded me.
Back in the backyard where I first saw the sky through my
father's thatched roof, my village groans under my mother's
skirt birthing new hope in prayer for a child firm in his
ways as it carry my umbilical on green banana leaves and
the scented aroma of village songs now fading into the
dusty thirst of warmth from a familiar smile. Eyes accuse
my paranoid senses and it jump in nightmarish fever
whenever a siren rings its ominous sound. Madness is a
constant threat as shadows overwhelm daylight cornering it
with harsh whispers of punishments of flame throwers onto
my swollen feet and numb hands.
The next maternity ward aligned for my next rebirth and
baptism is a grey room manned by grey suited men with

106

faces long death of emotions. And the cesarean section they intend to perform is as crude as an amateur abortionist in a hurry.

What is left of my old decency and pride is crudely paraded on the cold operating table as men size my life's worth with biased scales perhaps from Shylock's days. Help was alluded to without insurance or guarantee. Safety was mentioned in an undertone so i missed the term. But I came out dripping a cold near death sweat with a number like all patients must. I had arrived at the altar of earthly saving shore, and I had acquired a new name to add to all the odd ones of the past.

My name in full then is Birthright Exchange. Exchange took my surname and clan name. A born again, baptized vagabond just got a new name and home. Except, there is a price. The price of up rootedness is the cold feeling of life standing out in the frozen snow replaying life before truth became a dangerous topic to the ears of malfunctioning States back where democracies are still in nursery schools.

The mark of the hunted is in the ring of my new name. And a name carrying the character of its bearer drones on in silent torment as time sweetly echoes old tales of the cost of a tongue to the ears of goons that live and act as gods in their appointed times and territories. Knowing me my dozen names as boarders define me, restlessness sends me to the solitude of own company to militate against failing to respond to the call of myself on demand. I have become a spy on me as others are. I spy on my moods and my mental status. I spy on my location; I spy on faces especially if too familiar. I spy on everything and everybody, and boy! Are there enemies!

I see them and hear them rushing to uncover the real in the unreal. I feel them creeping to pounce on me to reveal the cluster of baptism names so far accrued. I sense them stalking me in my dreams waiting to trace my dialect and send me back to the hell recently escaped from.

Am so very tired. I have a craving for normal. I just want to take a walk and feel the sun on my face. I miss bursting into spontaneous song just because. I wish to call a friend and laugh at life. But I can't. For I am a sinner in the eyes of my landlord. And sinners such as I have been declared, are punished by being deleted from living and their memories faded by being refused a burial.

So here I am. A born again human with an identity crisis like an old spy who believed his lies. Am cursing life as I eat with a mumble under my foul breath. I think of my lover and spit at the sky convinced she smiles at my tormentors as a measure of gaining favor against harassment.

I am born again and bear a new name, but am far from whole, with all the holes punched on my psyche by this journey to the unknown. This process of my resurrection is digging me in deeper into a different detention camp. The only positive is I get to chronicle my spiral to where this ends, unlike my malevolent accusers who suffers, that I still breathe.

Yes. I still breathe the wind piloting me to the next bus stop of this life where I found a mango seed I flung out the window in a fate of distasteful and displaced anger sprout. I stopped in my tracks. I stared in utter disbelief at life fighting to stay afloat at the oddest of places. I went closer to check out this miracle of rejection turning to acceptance and daring to take chances.

The seed had lost the outer covering in the hostile manner of its rejection. What will eventually be the root shot out tenderly in form of a fading yellowish green tendril reaching down the edge of the stone where the mother seed hung on with nothing but the will to die so tomorrow the next generation of mangoes would have a chance to feed humanity?

I was ashamed of my anger that robbed this kindly nurturer of humanity and wildlife a proper positioning for the purpose for which it now struggled.

I had walked a rough road for many a mile. There are nights when I wasn't sure I would see light of day. I had run and sprinted from ghosts out to harm me. Now, a seed was lending its lesson on resilience in a language that knows never to give up.

The seeds concern is not that with disgust it was flung out with a bitter hand. Its purpose was to die so more mangoes could be born. Incapable of placing itself in a fertile place for better chances of survivor, it stoically reached out from the ledge of a rocky parch and send hope of growth through the thin threads of shoots.

And I knew then, what I know now. That am not owed comfort by my persecutors. That if I live or die is not their concern. That how I chose to live from now is not dependent on those who sent me here but on me.

And I, was once more, born again. This time, the rebirth was physically and emotionally painfully personal.

I knew I was not a hero neither a worm. I realized that I had been selfish and unforgiving.

I saw me for whom I had become. A grumpy soul who focused on the injuries I had accrued and not the healing I could embrace by moving on.

Then, from a distance, thunder rolled with a deafening roar. Some fat raindrops drummed on the roof top like kids playing male drums. I looked at my teacher and Baptist, the

111

quiet mango seed, and something passed between the two of us. We are each a brother's keeper. And as rain pelted the roof more furiously now, I reached out and covered the little tendrils with enough soil to ground the seed to grow. Then, I went back to the veranda of this home away from home facing my cowardly old eyes with the reborn eyes of a creature equal with all other creatures big and small.

Yes. A man defines his circumstances. That's the wisdom of progress of rebirth taught by the silence of a mango seed.

And while I packed my duffle bag for the next location, I bid goodbye most earnestly to my tutor and mentor from the warm blanket of soil I had heaped on her.

WELCOME TO MY ISLAND: Thrashing out the truth.

In the land, where senselessness rules, a man is lonely if he embraces truth. For truth, is a dark bird, that should melt with the night shadows. His home is his mind on an island way away from the float some debris of brokenness and the stench of betrayal that characterizes the running Bazaar of men death of consciousness.

Welcome to the Continent of contractual maladies of overripe pretenses. Here, you stand short before the court of mass abusers. Blame is apportioned to the blameless. Character is the first casualty in finishing off a man before generic products from the lands of biological warfare, bears and pandas are fed into your system so your death certificate can be colored with some known end.

Sons of freedom strugglers are castrated. Their balls squeezed with party pliers till they squeal with hoarse voices of ghosts of dead bones in the dungeons of their tormented minds. A place to rest the broken ribs is on caves in the Misty Mountains where gorilla's and baboons shyly

113

skirt around the two legged affair with a demented mind cursing the gods of truth. The only song afloat in the Fevered mind of a displaced soul is the song of lamentations that rolls down the forest floor like giant Lianas without trees to hang their mossy coats on.

Welcome to the Countries where death is no longer a threat but a way of life and predictable like known religious dates. Here the stalker and the enemy is one and the same, perhaps joined in unholy matrimony or by kinship matrix. The philosophy of man having a price is heavily subsidized with incentives all green and crispy in quantities enough to keep drinks flowing for weeks.

Welcome to the realms of social policing that rapes reality of the sufferers in the same fashion as the state rapist. The language and status is capital letters giving it a "stand alone etiquettes" like baptism of a swine with a clean name hoping to change its exuberant past time with dirt and stench. As they say in rural villages long used to speaking in crypt tongues, "washing a free range chickens legs is a mission in futility". NGOs once had a missionary mission in lands where bias needed to walk straight paths. No longer. They now eat with the Lions, scavenge with buzzards and weeps with the endangered rhinos.

Money being a leveler of uneven grounds, heaps of it has narrowed the narrative of the persecuted to read dissident in quotes.

Where then does truth go to tell it's two cents of observed and experienced traumas of being alive in the world of monkeys who are too fat to swing the trees? Where does truth stand to recount injuries of the land and victims of deprivation when the crocodile is the judge of truth about all those whom he swallowed as they attempted to Cross the river of poverty?

Where does truth pitch it's tent to make a report of those the soil covers in unmarked graves if open sewers are the resting places of tongues that went into the good night at midday in organized kidnappings ?

Welcome to the space where paradox parades it's poachers of piety replacing it with pitiable fallacy's of plunder and mayhem on truth Sayers and gets away with it because corruption has become the heartbeat of a nation recruiting all who wish to earn a quick buck for a piece of indecency.

So truth is marooned into an island where it earns the term, "terminally insane."

There, it's left to slowly disintegrate into bits of Monologues bitterly contesting inner voices that once swam in clean waters before being flung into the central unnatural order of disorder where wrongs rights nothing and hope is measured by ability to swim with sharks eventually all the way to the belly and out as pellets of shit Into an ocean so dark, even the saintly sun shies to shine it's light knowing the devil lives in the deep of schemers like worms in a cadaver.

Way out then is the lonely path of vagabond entities, scurrying under the radar less sky, riding on a prayer and resilience of an explorer to where sense listen and offers a respite from the scorching jabs of men whose souls got bought by an unrepentant revolution gone mad.

A man becomes an Island carrying his truth away from where it could benefit the loser's.

And in his heart, he chants an old saying.

"Truth never dies even if I do"

And a soul rides on the waves of the universe, carrying its shell of pasts shrunken dreams. Stepping gingery on the Rocky paths of guessed paths and dark corners, trusting Providence with utmost faith. To suffer uprooted-ness is a tragedy many just read about and marvel at the victim's resilience in the face of foggy presentations of realities so fearful, insanity is a constant companion. Dressed in loneliness, drunk on anxiety, every shadow draws a dagger to draw blood. Every sound is amplified footsteps of a pursuing foe. Every breath is drawn with calculation lest it's too loud to draw attention to its location. Constantly on edge, paranoia settles into a pattern that persists even in sleep. A restlessness settles on the nerves wrecking further havoc on a body poorly fed. To run is then the only option and woe is the soul that knows not the way of sincere prayers or the reliance on guiding hands from the unknown where whips rain on known locales. To hide is no longer a game or jest for enemies real and imagined plague the surroundings prompting irrational and rational to collide into a fantasia of erratic moves in jerky coordination. At this plane, goings on in the mind are heated debates extolling options not taken and what could have been had silence won over telling of truth.

A prophet is a lonely soul often encumbered by the weight of his message which he never has the luxury of not telling. Such are the few who die en-route searching for a safe haven from the hellish lands where truth never grows roots. Such are the few who run to see tomorrow's sun from caving dungeons away in the middle of the unknown holding prayers as an anthem for hope. Such are the few who bravery and courage set apart for persecution at home and who by the grace of the purity of the universe and it's respect of truth, presents miracles from the most unlikely of places.

Whether tagged a " runaway"

Whether ratted a "fugitive"

Truth never bowed to coercion.

Truth is a hero in hiding or in the open

Truth is resident of life and not a visitor

Truth is a master and servant and cannot be denied

Truth never rusts however long it's imprisoned

Truth is a judge and counsel.

Truth never sleeps even when it's Carrier does. It's the reason why,from the heart of a stranger whose second names is a battle for the tongue to pronounce, hope is dropped onto the lap of a fleeing spirit, to at once feel the human connection of care and empathy. And hope rises once more. Bitterness recedes and the mission of truth sits a little fairly. Perhaps a smile from a warm meal. Perhaps a tear for gratitude. Perhaps a griping yearning to hear a familiar voice of love. Perhaps a lot more......but for the moment, the cloud has cleared. Running has slowed to a walk and the feel of the sun is on the skin warming deeper.

Yes. Man is a worse monster to his own than a hostile ghost. He casts out his own to die in the deserts of unknown terrains to keep truth of his less than clean ways away from those he rules. Corruption has become an evil religion whose followers thrive on murder of any and all bearers of truth.

But man too, is a savior of his own kind. A stranger relating to another stranger as a fellow human. A feeling that rises to feed and clothe one bare of basics.

Yes. Man is his own ill and his cure

One casts, one catches.

One Chase's, one places,

And the world rolls on, parts with blinkers shading their innocence from the needs of those unfortunate to live under the terror of maniacal schemers of dictatorships, who murder as punishment for truth told, and those who feel every pain of a fellow human suffering the "crime of telling the truth"

This balance of Providence against the pathetic shenanigans of thugs masquerading as leaders of men is what gives hope to humanity that TRUTH, may have a lofty price for its teller to pay, but it's the ONLY way it knows to operate.

For those Truth choses as its mouthpiece, history has sad Chronicles, even tragic, but lessons abide about the indomitable spirit of truth that remain restless till it rises to tell its bit regardless of the consequences.

For the prophets who bear the scars of carrying the burden of telling the truth, let the universe speak to more strangers on your path to stand in the gap.

A man is an island and the island is man. Both are the universe. Each is complete. Both are completely companionable. Truth is the fruit that feeds the companionship to a fair world. If only more could embrace it?

HARSH REALITIES

When chickens sprout claws and chase the eagle up the
misty mountain, the corner has turned the road and normal
is redefined. Shouted whispers armed with lethal prayers
are unleashed at the naked torso of a man, whose crime is
spotting the looters of the lone old lady's granary, leaving
her myriad orphaned grandchildren with emptiness for
dinner. Her acidic inner tears cough curses behind cupped
hands as she coaxes the dying brood to rest in peace. What
is stolen, is then sent to the market for the moneyed to fill
their carts and celebrate the independence of a Nation.
An itchiness wraps the land with a grandiose malady of
anxiety and paranoia for the eyes of state hoots everywhere
assessing the hearts of the masses for disloyalty. The music
of the land has turned to a one liner in praise of a
uniformed gravestone dressed in military fatigues. Even
empty farts of the quarreling bowels must be timed to
resonate with the loving tribute of the figure looming over
the dry dreams of ruler ship. A time of it, the dwellers of
this land has. Daily, served with weighty slogans, in praise

of structures bent by the wind of gluttony, they watch in resignation as every rural youth runs across the border searching for sense and direction to a full stomach.

Africa, the land of mystery and the bucket list of many a foreigner, yours, is a case of rot trading insults with vulgarity. You have been set up by outside drama kings of commercial shenanigans and now you are setting yourselves up. The irony is not lost on your coarse manner in which you treat your fellow kin. Your hand is rough and your manner immoral. Your heart is darker than your night sky's on a moonless night. You are drunk on the ideas imported from lands that know not to respect creator. Blaming the past is a past time and preoccupation akin to prescription intake of medication.. The only news welcome to your elephant ears specially tuned to hear dissenting voices is a deal where you earn more than the economy of older Nations. Largesse is your middle name and spares nothing and no one when it comes to grander.

Africa, your name is a shocking pronunciation in decent society. You rape your own without shame and invest where others provide security. You cripple every effort of social growth fearing your exposure by opened senses. You imprison the voices of truth and murder protesters. You sponsor battles and wars against unarmed masses. You bring your people to their knees through ignorance and denial. Your only class is repeated mantras of the rising star of ' your Nation' even as the world looks on in horror.

Africa, when shall you awake to the fact that the truth has no price and that greed is a short holiday before time catches it with the proverbial fire, purges it and shames it, sending a story for history to chronicle?

Africa, the land of giant mines, rich forests and magnificent wildlife, what other blessing do you need when you mismanage the very resources others covet?

The very brains you chase across borders for their truth are the very priests that would have presided over the senses of your sickly mind, healing it enough for you to see the insanity of your ways. Past the jungle of netting goons, your sons find welcome respite in soils away from their hearth. They brood over lost times and relationships even as they toil to stay alive. They survive. They thrive. And make names for themselves thousands of miles away from

124

where their umbilical cord weeps with yearnings for the footsteps of lost sons. As you spit nonstop at the news of their success, having shorn your followers of any and all sense of truth making them fear to tell anything close to reality, you continue your marauding verbosity that makes for sad entertainment at news hours in your own media, which if you cared to check, airs to emptiness in the homes of those you assume are your faithful's.

A dictator is a sick and wounded skunk whose stench is only accommodated by fellow skunks and vultures who thrive on the dead and dying. He loves his own stories and jokes and misses the well camouflaged yawns and embarrassed looks of those in attendance.

Then, there is the opposition politics. Lol!

Another lot of voices with eyes on what's wrong but with no plan on how to make the wrong right, and if they have, the chance is crippled in marred protests as they try their hand at contesting the tick on the tit at statehouse. Theatre of the absurd is the daily show in most of our beloved states. With pockets lined with promissory notes at deals to be sealed upon succeeding in a coup or bought and botched elections, confusion is the ration to the nation each tribe pitted against the other in the quest of looting and not governance.

Which way for Africa really? Which way for its people who are pawned at their homes and streets by lawlessness masquerading as law keepers? Which way for a people who knows not which way the sun will rise tomorrow and whose tune shall be embraced?

Africa, the land of much is married to less which is lessening by the day. With leaderships whose allegiance is to self-first, then the sponsors of the seat which sit the leader, the land breeds continuously with a narrative that reads like a never ending dirge.

Africa, you lament at the bent of your story told by foreign mouths, but check the faces of those you gore on the heads with yet unpaid bullets for telling it as it is. Which angle does their mistreatment, arbitrary arrests, imprisonment without trial and even death under a ghastly cloud of mischief tell? How else does death from lack of medicines and hunger can be told except as it were? Militarizing social interactions where each is afraid of the next and the death of human camaraderie can only be told by the silent tongues and opaque staring eyes. And they tell much, those who suffer in silence. They tell much those who ride the nights under fire from your goons, they tell much those who rely on bush treatment for their ills. They tell much those who follow you as you abuse their manhood for a morsel and stale beer leftovers from your high table. They tell much those who see your motorcade snaking around town with top of the range fuel guzzler while TB wracking lungs wheeze at the road sides to cheer your dead soul to your next mission of visionless leadership.

Africa, the land of diversity and resilient souls, when shall you learn to be your own men and stand for what is right even if it's the neighbor playing truant with his kin. You have mirrored the world and come up with prefects capable of predicting treads of upcoming disasters. Why then,

do you, like everyone else of less concern do you wait till the rapist is through the wreckage of life before arriving for talks armed with first aid bandage for the deep gushes of inflicted injuries? Are these fine institutions for window dressing to show the world you live in a modern bungalow or is there more? If there is more, what is it and where has it worked and what are the results for earning mileage and allowances besides the hefty salaries? Perhaps its job creation for the elderly and the relations of their sweethearts to loot from the wider continent under guise of Africanism. One has to wonder why a distant figure takes human interest in a human who is thrown to the dogs by his own, for that is the fate of Africa with those either insane enough to stand to the truth, or foolish enough to dare it knowing the consequences.

Africa, the land of beautiful drum beats and majestic sunrises only rivalled by their sunsets. When shall you ever sit long enough to read the history of what brings you to where you are? Politics has no friendships but a whore serving for a moment for a fee. Politicking has a price and when it involves you trading with the devil you must know he is worse than shylock. He shall come calling. This time not for repayment but for your soul and soil.

Africa, Once upon a time, when your eyes only knew the truth, a stranger came calling. He hoodwinked you, stole your wit and your children. Another has come calling. This one has a magic purse and rains on your every wish with a sly eye. As you smile all the way to a numbered account and palatial homes far away from your beggary populace, remember this. The man you bludgeon for telling the truth is not the enemy, neither is he after you or your raw power. He is the hope of the land you are dispossessing. He is the voice of those you have silenced. And like all who are dead to truth, your day is well on its way. What shall your defense be when the deadness you have blanketed your people with wear off?

Manufactured by Amazon.ca
Bolton, ON

18115474R00077